PROBABILITY

Dice and Cards

Carlo Di Carlo

Introduction:

Probability is a branch of study in Statistics. A probability is the chance that an uncertain outcome will occur. We often refer to outcomes as events. Probabilities are always between 0 and 1 inclusive. When we say inclusive, that means the probability could be equal to 0, and the probability could be equal to 1. A probability of 1 means that there is a 100% chance of that outcome occurring. A probability of 0 means there is a 0% chance of that outcome occurring. For instance, a probability of .5 means that there is a 50% chance of that outcome occurring. A probability of .0377 means there is a 3.77% chance of the outcome occurring. Statisticians, however, often use probabilities instead of percentages to express uncertainties. It is often crucial to know the probabilities of events/outcomes occurring because this will help us in evaluating decisions, when there is uncertainty. In Statistics, events/outcomes take on the values of A, B, C, D, etc. (uppercase letters). When we want to find the probability of an event occurring we often write this as:

P(A) = Probability of event A occurring

The probability of any event A is between 0 and 1 inclusive.

0 <= P(A) <= 1

Rules of Probability:

P(A) = (# outcomes satisfying A / Total # Outcomes)

not Rule

P(not A) = 1 - P(A)

The probability that event A does not occur is 1 minus the probability of A.   See the Venn Diagram below. A Venn diagram is a way to represent a Sample Space (all possible outcomes). The area in the entire Venn diagram sums to 1, which means it covers all possible outcomes.

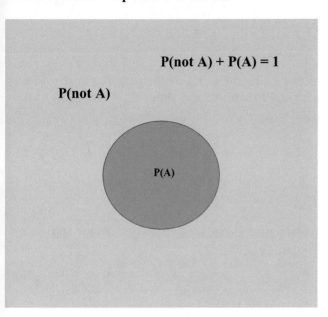

General Addition Rule

$$P(A \text{ or } B) = P(A) + P(B) - P(A \text{ and } B)$$

The probability of A or B occurring is equal to the Probability of A plus the Probability of B, minus the Probability of A and B occurring.

General Addition Rule if Outcomes are Mutually Exclusive (Non-overlapping)

$$P(A \text{ or } B) = P(A) + P(B)$$

If A and B are mutually exclusive then the Probability of A or B equals the Probability of A plus the probability of B.

General Addition Rule for Independent Events

$$P(A \text{ or } B) = P(A) + P(B) - P(A)P(B)$$

If A and B are independent, then the Probability of A or B equals the Probability of A plus the probability of B, minus the Probability of A times the Probability of B.

Multiplication Rule

$$P(A \text{ and } B) = P(A)P(B|A)$$

The Probability of A and B equals the probability of A times the conditional probability of B given that A has already occurred.

Mutually Exclusive (non-overlapping) Events

$$P(A \text{ and } B) = 0$$

If two events A and B are mutually exclusive (they cannot occur together) then the Probability of A and B equals zero.

Independence (Rule # 1)

$$P(A \text{ and } B) = P(A)P(B)$$

If two events A and B are independent then the Probability of A and B equals the Probability of A times the Probability of B.

Independence (Rule # 1) For 3 Events

$$P(A \text{ and } B \text{ and } C) = P(A)P(B)P(C)$$

If three events A, B and C are independent of each other then the Probability of A and B and C equals the Probability of A times the Probability of B times the Probability of C.

Independence (Rule # 2)

$$P(A|B) = P(A)$$

If A and B are independent (A and B do not affect each other), then the Probability of A given that B has already occurred is equal to the Probability of A.

Statistical Experiments:
Tossing Coins

Tossing 1 coin:

A typical probabilistic experiment conducted in Statistics includes tossing coins. With a coin there are 2 possible outcomes, Heads and Tails. The sample space for tossing a coin represents all possible outcomes (2 equally likely outcomes). We write the sample space for tossing one fair coin as follows:

{ Heads, Tails} or {H, T}   (where H = Heads, T = Tails)

When we talk about a fair coin in Statistics, this means P(Heads) = P(Tails) = .5

Tossing 2 coins:

If we toss 2 fair coins the sample space is as follows (4 equally likely outcomes) and is of the format
(1st toss, 2nd toss):

{ (H, T) (T, H) (T, T) (H, H) }

Tossing 3 coins:

If we toss 3 fair coins the sample space is as follows (8 equally likely outcomes) and is of the format
(1st toss, 2nd toss, 3rd toss):

{ (H, H, H) (H, H, T) (H, T, T) (H, T, H) (T, T, T) (T, T, H) (T, H, H) (T, H, T) }

Tossing 4 coins:

If we toss 4 fair coins the sample space is as follows (16 equally likely outcomes) and is of the format
(1st toss, 2nd toss, 3rd toss, 4th toss):

{ (H, H, H, H) (H,H, H, T) (H, H, T, T) (H, H, T, H) (H, T, T, T) (H, T, T, H)
(H, T, H, H) (H, T, H, T) (T, H, H, H) (T, H, H, T) (T, H, T, T) (T, H, T, H)
(T, T, T, T) (T, T, T, H) (T, T, H, H) (T, T, H, T)}

Tossing n coins in general:

If we toss n coins in general there are 2^n possible equally likely outcomes.

When we toss:

1 coin -> $2^1 = 2$ equally likely outcomes

2 coins -> 2^2 = 4 equally likely outcomes
3 coins -> 2^3 = 8 equally likely outcomes
4 coins -> 2^4 = 16 equally likely outcomes

Example 1: You toss a fair coin one time.

   a) What is the probability it lands Tails?

There are only 2 possible equally likely outcomes when you toss a coin once: {H, T}. Since it is a fair coin, this means half the time it will land on Tails, so P(Tails) = .5

b) What is the probability it lands Heads?

Once again, it is a fair coin, so the probability it lands heads is P(Heads) = .5

Example 2: You toss a fair coin 2 times. What is the probability of getting 2 tails?

Let's write out the possible outcomes once again:

{ (H, T) (T, H) (T, T) (H, H) }

This represents 4 equally likely outcomes for tossing a fair coin twice

The only way to get 2 tails is to get the outcome (T, T) which is 1 out of 4 equally likely outcomes, so P(2 tails) = ¼ = 0.25

Example 3: You toss a fair coin 3 times.

   a) What is the probability of getting 2 heads and 1 tail?

There are 8 equally likely outcomes when you toss a coin three times:

{ (H, H, H) (H, H, T) (H, T, T) (H, T, H) (T, T, T) (T, T, H) (T, H, H) (T, H, T) }

You can get: (H, H, T) or (H, T, H) or (T, H, H)

There are 3 out of 8 equally likely outcomes resulting in 2 heads and 1 tail.

P(2 Heads, 1 Tail) = 3/8 = 0.375

b) **What is the probability of getting tails on the 3rd toss?**

Once again there are 8 equally likely possible outcomes.

There are 4 outcomes which satisfy the criteria of tails on the third toss.

(H, H, T) or (H, T, T) or (T, H, T) or (T, T, T)

Therefore, P(tails on 3rd toss) = 4/8 = 0.5

Example 4: You toss a fair coin 4 times.

a) **What is the probability of getting 4 tails**

There is only 1 way to get 4 tails in 4 tosses. You have to get (T, T, T, T) and there are 16 possible outcomes so the probability is 1/16.

b) **What is the probability of getting 3 Heads and 1 Tail in 4 tosses.**

You can get (H, H, H, T) or (H, H, T, H) or (H, T, H, H) or (T, H, H, H). These are 4 equally likely outcomes out of 16 possible outcomes.
4/16 = ¼ = 0.25

Rolling Dice
Rolling 1 die:

Another common probabilistic experiment used in Statistics is rolling dice. Typically we talk about rolling a fair 6-sided die.

When we roll a fair 6-sided die one time, we are equally likely to get any of the numbers 1 through 6.

P(roll 1) = P(roll 2) = P(roll 3) = P(roll 4) = P(roll 5) = P(roll 6) = 1/6

The sample space (all possible outcomes) is as follows:

{ 1, 2, 3, 4, 5, 6}

Rolling 2 dice:

When we roll 2 fair dice, there are 36 possible outcomes. We can draw a chart for the sum of 2 dice as follows which shows all possible outcomes:

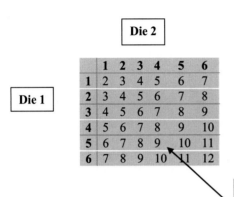

Each square represents the sum of two dice:
$(5, 4) \rightarrow 5 + 4 = 9$

We can also look at the sample space for rolling 2 fair dice as all 36 possible outcomes in terms of pairs of dice of the form (1ˢᵗ die, 2ⁿᵈ die) as follows:

{ (1, 1) (1, 2) (1, 3) (1, 4) (1, 5) (1, 6)
  (2, 1) (2, 2) (2, 3) (2, 4) (2, 5) (2, 6)
  (3, 1) (3, 2) (3, 3) (3, 4) (3, 5) (3, 6)
  (4, 1) (4, 2) (4, 3) (4, 4) (4, 5) (4, 6)
  (5, 1) (5, 2) (5, 3) (5, 4) (5, 5) (5, 6)
  (6, 1) (6, 2) (6, 3) (6, 4) (6, 5) (6, 6) }

Example 4:

You roll a fair 6-sided die.

    a) What is the probability you roll an even number?

        Let A = roll an even #

P(A) = P(roll an even #) = 3/6

Simply count the # of even outcomes (2, 4 and 6 are even #'s) and divide by the total # of outcomes.

b) What is the probability you roll a 5 or higher?

Let $A = \text{roll} \geq 5$

$P(A) = P(\text{roll} \geq 5) = 2/6 = 1/3$

If we can roll a 5 or higher on 1 die, that means we can roll a 5 or a 6. This represents 2 possible outcomes satisfying A (roll ≥ 5) out of 6 possible outcomes.

Example 5: You roll 2 fair 6-sided dice. Find the sample spaces (all possible outcomes) for the following:

a) The second die is twice the first die
   The only outcomes which satisfy this are { (1, 2) , (2, 4) and (3,6)}

b) The 1ˢᵗ die and 2ⁿᵈ die are both even

   The outcomes which satisfy this are:

   { (2, 2) (2, 4) (2, 6)
    (4, 2) (4, 4) (4, 6)
    (6, 2) (6, 4) (6, 6) }

c) The second die is less than 2

   If the second die is less than 2 it must be equal to 1, so the outcomes satisfying this are:

   { (1, 1) (2, 1) (3, 1) (4, 1) (5, 1) (6, 1) }

Example 6: You roll 2 fair dice.

a) What is the probability you roll a sum of 9?

The first thing we can do is look at the chart for the sum of 2 dice. We can also write out the pairs of dice which sum to 9.

Die 2

Die 1

	1	2	3	4	5	6
1	2	3	4	5	6	7
2	3	4	5	6	7	8
3	4	5	6	7	8	9
4	5	6	7	8	9	10
5	6	7	8	9	10	11
6	7	8	9	10	11	12

These cells all sum to 9

There are 4 outcomes which sum to 9 out of 36 possible outcomes, which means that the probability is as follows:

P(roll a sum of 9) = 4/36

We can also look at the pairs of dice. The possible pairs which sum to 9 are (3, 6) (6, 3) (4, 5) and (5, 4) which is once again 4 out of 36 outcomes.

b) What is the probability you roll a sum of 9 or higher?

If we get a sum of 9 or higher, this means we can roll a sum of 9, 10, 11, or 12

Die 2

	1	2	3	4	5	6
1	2	3	4	5	6	7
2	3	4	5	6	7	8
3	4	5	6	7	8	9
4	5	6	7	8	9	10
5	6	7	8	9	10	11
6	7	8	9	10	11	12

Die 1 (label at left of table)

These cells all sum to 9 or higher

There are 10 outcomes in the chart which represent a sum of 9 or higher. We can also look at each possible roll separately.

$$P(\text{roll} >= 9) = P(\text{roll } 9) + P(\text{roll } 10) + P(\text{roll } 11) + P(\text{roll } 12)$$

$$4/36 \quad + \quad 3/36 \quad + \quad 2/36 \quad + \quad 1/36 \quad = \quad 10/36$$

We can also look at the pairs of dice.

Ways to get a 9: (4,5), (5,4), (6,3) and (3,6) →   P(roll 9) = 4/36

Ways to get a 10: (6,4), (4,6) and (5,5) →   P(roll 10) = 3/36

Ways to get an 11: (5,6), (6,5) → P(roll 11) =   2/36

Ways to get a 12: (6,6) →   P(roll 12) = 1/36

c) What is the probability you roll a sum of 5 or a sum of 7?

First let's look at the chart for the sum of 2 dice.

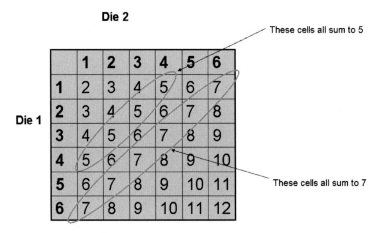

Since you can't roll a sum of 5 and a sum of 7 at the same time on 2 dice, then 5 and 7 are mutually exclusive outcomes -> P(roll 5 and roll 7) = 0. In general, outcomes with dice are mutually exclusive. Apply the General Addition Rule if the results are mutually exclusive.

$$P(A \text{ or } B) = P(A) + P(B)$$

P(roll 5 or roll 7) = P(roll 5) + P(roll 7)

4/36 + 6/36 = 10/36

By looking at the chart for the sum of 2 dice we can see that there are four outcomes which sum to 5 and six outcomes which sum to 7. This is 10 out of 36 possible outcomes. Remember, we can also write out the possible pairs of dice.

Ways to get a 5: (3,2) (2, 3) (4,1) and (1, 4) →   P(roll 5) = 4/36

Ways to get a 7: (6, 1) (1, 6) (5, 2) (2, 5) (3, 4) (4, 3)
                                            →   P(roll 7) = 6/36

Cards

When talking about probabilities involving playing cards, we usually talk about a standard deck of 52 cards.

-There are four suits with 13 cards for each suit:
(♣ = clubs, ♠ = spades, ♥ = hearts ♦ = diamonds)
-There are 2 colors, with 26 cards of each color: (red, black)
-There are 4 of each card rank: (Aces, Kings, Queens, Jacks, 10's, 9's, …..2's)
-There are 1 of each card rank and suit combination (Ace of clubs,…etc.)

If you are drawing 1 card-> Below are the probabilities associated with a standard deck of 52 cards:

➔ **P(clubs) = P(spades) = P(hearts) = P(diamonds) = 13/52**

➔ **P(red) = P(black) = 26/52**

➔ **P(Ace) = P(King) = P(Queen) = P(Jack) = P(10) = P(9) = …… = P(2) = 4/52**

➔ **P(Ace of clubs) = P(King of Clubs) = ….. = P(2 of diamonds) = 1/52**

With vs. Without Replacement
We can draw cards with replacement, which means we put the card back in the deck and shuffle the deck after we draw each card. Shuffling the deck insures that we are selecting

cards at random. In this scenario, trials are independent. What we draw on the first card, does not affect what we draw on the second card. What we draw on the second card does not affect what we draw on the third card, etc. When we draw without replacement, we do not put the cards back in the deck before we draw another card. This means that trials are dependent upon each other (not independent) and involve a series of conditional probabilities.

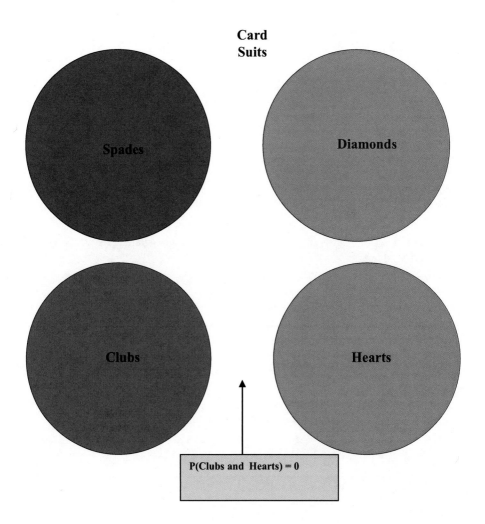

When playing cards it is important to realize that none of the suits overlap. The suits are mutually exclusive of each other. For instance, if you draw one card, P(diamonds AND clubs) = 0. Diamonds do not overlap with clubs. They also don't overlap with spades or hearts. Also, red cards don't overlap with black cards.

Example 7 : **The following question involves using a standard deck of 52 cards. Find the probabilities of the following:**

a) P(Ace or King) (1 card)

   First, let's draw a Venn diagram for this probability.

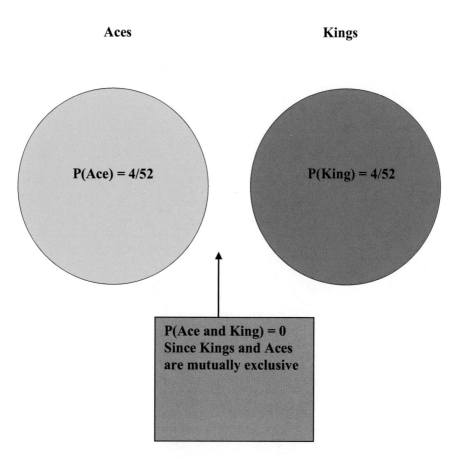

Aces

Kings

P(Ace) = 4/52

P(King) = 4/52

P(Ace and King) = 0
Since Kings and Aces
are mutually exclusive

As you can see from the Venn diagram above, Aces and Kings don't overlap which means they are mutually exclusive. We use the General Addition Rule below when events are mutually exclusive:

P(A or B) = P(A) + P(B)

Therefore, P(Ace or King) = P(Ace) + P(King) = **4/52 + 4/52 = 8/52** = .1538

b) **P(King or Clubs)**

   Once again, let's draw out the Venn Diagram.

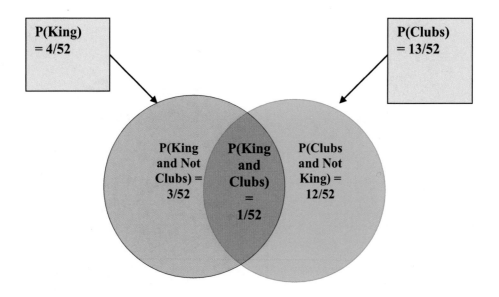

Using the General Addition Rule for 2 events we have:

$$P(A \text{ or } B) = P(A) + P(B) - P(A \text{ and } B)$$

P(King or Clubs) = P(King) + P(Clubs) – P(King and Clubs)

$$= \ 4/52 \ + 13/52 \ - 1/52 = \ 16/52 = \ .3077$$

c) P(Queen or Black Card)
   Below is the Venn Diagram

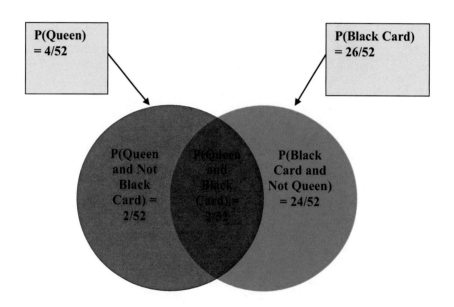

Once again, we can use the General Addition Rule:

P(A or B) = P(A) + P(B) – P(A and B)

P(Queen or Black) = P(Queen) + P(Black) − P(Queen and Black)

$$= \quad 4/52 \quad + 26/52 \quad - \quad 2/52 \quad = \quad 28/52 = .5385$$

d) What is the probability of drawing a King, followed by a Queen, followed by a 7, without replacement?

When we say followed by that means that these events have to occur in sequence (in order), so we have to multiply the probabilities together. After we draw a King, there are still four Queens left, because we haven't drawn any Queens yet. After we draw the Queen, there are still four 7's left, since we haven't drawn any 7's previously. The denominator decreases by 1 each time because we draw without replacement.

$P(King)P(Queen)P(7) =$

$(4/52)(4/51)(4/50) = .000483$

e) What is the probability of drawing 3 Aces in a row (without replacement)?

Since it is without replacement, the denominator will decrease by one each time we draw a new card. After we draw the first Ace, there is one less Ace left in the deck, so now there are three Aces. After we draw the second Ace, there are two Aces left.

We have to find:
1st draw   2nd   3rd
$P(Ace)P(Ace)P(Ace) =$

$(4/52)(3/51)(2/50) = .000181$

f)   What is the probability of drawing 3 Aces in a row (with replacement)?

Since it is with replacement, it is like starting over again each time we draw a new card. The probability of Ace on the first draw is 4 out of 52.

After we draw a card, we put it back in the deck and shuffle. The probability of drawing an ace on the next draw is the same, since we started with a completely shuffled deck of cards.

1st   2nd   3rd
P(Ace)P(Ace)P(Ace)

(4/52)(4/52)(4/52) = .000455

g) What is the probability that the first time you draw an Ace is on the 5th draw? You draw cards without replacement.

First of all we have to realize what has to happen on the first 4 draws. You do not get an Ace on the first 4 draws. On the 5th draw there are still 4 Aces left because we have not drawn any Aces yet. Each time we draw another card there is one less card in the deck, since it is without replacement, therefore the denominator decreases by one each time we draw a new card.

P(not Ace)P(not Ace)P(not Ace)P(not Ace)P(Ace)
  1st draw   2nd draw   3rd draw   4th draw   5th draw

On the 1st draw, P(not Ace) = 1 – P(Ace) = 1 – 4/52 = 48/52

(48/52)(47/51)(46/50)(45/49)(4/48) = .0599

BlackJack

h) **In a standard game of blackjack, an Ace is worth 1 or 11 points, and a ten, Jack, Queen and King are worth 10 points. All other cards are worth their face value. You are dealt 2 cards, without replacement. What is the probability of being dealt 21 points.**

First, we have to consider all the possible ways of getting 21 points with two cards. If we get an Ace and we make it worth 11 points and then we get a card worth 10 points (10, Jack, Queen or King) that sums to 21 points.

We also have to consider the order in which the cards are drawn. We can get an Ace (11 points) on the first draw, and 10 points on the second draw or we can also get 10 points on the first draw, and an Ace (11 points) on the second draw.

There are four Aces, so the probability we draw an Ace on the 1st draw is just 4 out of 52. If we need to then draw 10 points on the 2nd draw we have:

$$P(A \text{ or } B) = P(A) + P(B)$$

$P(10 \text{ points on } 2^{nd} \text{ draw}) = P(10 \text{ or Jack or Queen or King}) =$

$P(10) + P(\text{Jack}) + P(\text{Queen}) + P(\text{King}) =$

$(4/51) + (4/51) + (4/51) + (4/51) = 16/51$

Keep in mind there are 51 cards left on the 2nd draw, because we already drew a card without replacement.

To solve this problem, we need to combine the general addition rule (OR rule) with the conditional probability rule (AND rule).

$$P(A \text{ or } B) = P(A) + P(B)$$

$$P(A \text{ and } B) = P(A)P(B|A)$$

So we have to solve:

| 1ST | 2nd | 1ST | 2nd |
| draw | draw | draw | draw |

P(Ace)P(10 points) or P(10 points)P(Ace) =

P(Ace)P(10 points) + P(10 points)P(Ace) =

(4/52)(16/51)   +   (16/52)(4/51)   = .0483

There is a 4.83% chance of being dealt 21 points with two cards in BlackJack!

DRAWING A FLUSH
i)
Find the probability of drawing a Flush of Hearts with a 5 card poker hand.

To draw a flush of Hearts that means all the cards you draw must be Hearts. (It doesn't necessarily mean that you have to draw a straight flush or a royal flush.)

Since there are 13 Hearts, you have 13 out of 52 cards that are Hearts on the first draw. On each subsequent draw (up to 5 cards) the denominator decreases by 1 because there is 1 less card overall to choose from, and the numerator decreases by 1 since there is 1 less heart left in the deck of cards.

Here is the probability:

1ˢᵗ draw 2ⁿᵈ   3ʳᵈ   4ᵗʰ   5ᵗʰ
(13/52)(12/51)(11/50)(10/49)(9/48) = .000495

This is about a 1 in 2,020 chance!

j)
Find the probability of being dealt a Flush in a 5 card poker hand in any suit.

Since it is symmetrical, the chance of being dealt a Flush in any suit would be 4 times the probability of being dealt a Flush of Hearts.

P(Flush of Hearts OR Spades OR Diamonds OR Clubs) =

4*P(flush of Hearts) = 4*(13/52)(12/51)(11/50)(10/49)(9/48) = .001980

This is about a 1 in 505 chance!

k) You are dealt 5 cards without replacement in a game of poker. What is the probability of being dealt a royal flush of hearts? (In order to get a royal flush of hearts, you need to get a 10, Jack, Queen, King and Ace of hearts. Look at the picture below.)

ROYAL FLUSH

There are 5 draws and you can get any of the 5 cards on the first draw. Thus there are 5 out of 52 possibilities on the first draw. On the next draw, assuming that you got one of the 5 cards you need, there are 4 cards left that you need, and 1 less card to choose from, which means there are 4 out of 51 possibilities. This continues until you draw the last card that you need to complete the royal flush of hearts.

(1st draw) (2nd) (3rd) (4th) (5th)
$$(5/52)(4/51)(3/50)(2/49)(1/48) = .0000003848$$

This is very unlikely. If we translate into percentage form (multiply the decimal by 100%), this will happen .00003848 % of the time. This is 3,848 times out of 10 billion! This translates to approximately a 1 out of 2,598,753 chance!!

BONUS QUESTION:

This question does not involve coins, dice, or cards but you can apply your knowledge of drawing cards without replacement to solve this problem!

An urn contains 7 red balls and 3 green balls. Find the probability of getting a red ball, followed by a green ball, followed by a red ball.
(without replacement). Below is the drawing of the initial state of the urn.

- On the first draw
- P(red) =

$$\frac{\#\,red}{\#\,red + \#\,green} = \frac{7}{7+3} = \frac{7}{10}$$

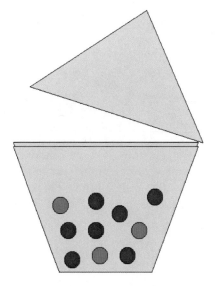

- A red ball is drawn on the 1st draw. Now there are 6 red balls left and all 3 green balls left.

  The probability of green on the 2nd draw is P(green) =

$$\frac{\#\,\mathbf{green}}{\#\,\mathbf{red} + \#\,\mathbf{green}} = \frac{3}{6+3} = \frac{3}{9}$$

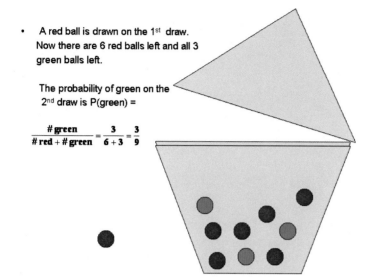

- A red ball is drawn on the 1st draw, and a green ball on the 2nd draw. Now there are 6 red balls left and 2 green balls left.

  The probability of red on the 3rd draw is P(red) =

$$\frac{\#\,\mathbf{red}}{\#\,\mathbf{red} + \#\,\mathbf{green}} = \frac{6}{6+2} = \frac{6}{8}$$

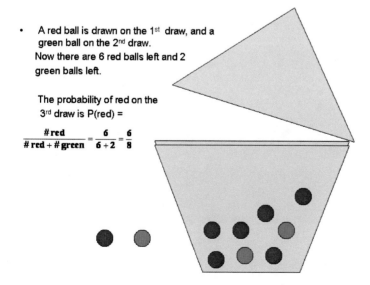

"Followed By" is a keyword that tells us these events have to occur is sequence or "In a row" which means we have to multiply (AND rule) the events together. The denominator decreases by 1 each time we draw a new ball because we do not put the balls back in the urn after we draw them, since it is without replacement. Putting all the parts together, from the 3 diagrams we have:

1st 2nd 3rd
Draw   Draw   Draw

P(red)P(green)P(red) =

(7/10)(3/9)(6/8)   = .175